Contents

Walking to school

On the way to school,
you walk past all kinds
of different houses.

These houses are new.
The bricks make interesting
shapes and patterns.

Over the railway

You cross a footbridge over the railway line to get to school. You can see tall blocks of flats in the distance.

There is a church near the school.
The children visit the church for harvest
festival and other special occasions.

Keeping safe

Yellow road markings tell cars not to park outside the school.

There is a bell and an entry phone on the gate for visitors.
What else can you see here that helps to keep children safe?

Welcome

You can look at the trees and flowers around the school entrance. They make the school look welcoming.

There is a warm welcome from
the school office, too.
What else can you see that
makes a visitor feel welcome?

In the classroom

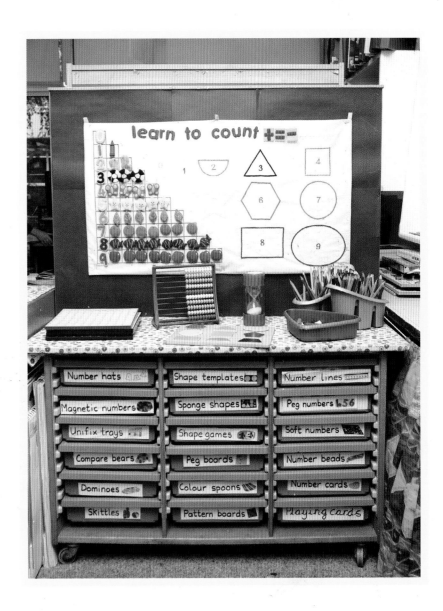

In the classroom, big windows let in plenty of light.
Does your classroom have the same equipment as this one?

Along the corridor

You can walk along the corridor, past the toilets ...

... and the children's coats.

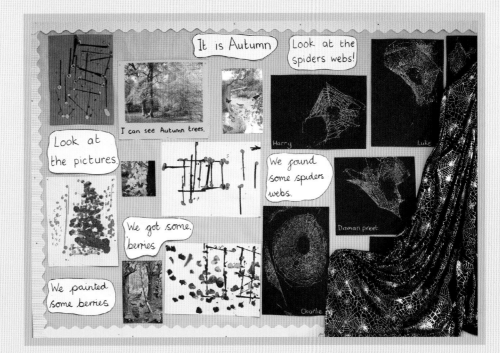

Children's work ...

... and a character from a book decorate the walls.

The playground

Outside, colourful wall paintings
brighten up the playground.
Who might have painted the pictures?

One part of the playground is grass.
Another part is concrete.

Looking after the school

The mother of one of the pupils
helps in the school garden.
What are the children growing?

The caretaker keeps the school clean and tidy. He mends things that are broken, too.

The school hall

Children eat their lunch at one end of the school hall.

Gym lessons take place at the other end.

What else takes place in your school hall?

The library

As well as lots of books, there are soft cushions, carpets and puppets in the library.

It is a good place to relax and read books at the end of the day.

Map

Follow the walk to school on the small map. Then, on the big map, put your finger on **Start** and trace the route around the school.

Key

office

head's office

hall

classroom

toilets

playground

garden

dining hall

canteen

library

PE cupboard

staff room

nursery

door

Start

School

Home

Quiz

The children walk past houses
on the way to school.
What else do they pass?

Look at pages 6, 7, 8 and 9.

Some children walk to school,
some come by car.
How else do children get
to school?

Look for a clue on page 6.

School furniture and equipment is
different from things at home.
What is specially made for
school?

Look at pages 14 to 25.

The children play outside at playtime.
    What games do they play?

Look at pages 18 and 19.

The caretaker looks after the school.
Who else works in the school?

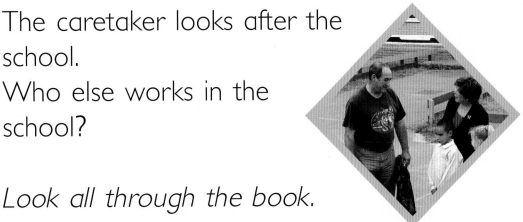

Look all through the book.

The school has a library.
    What are the other rooms in the school called?

Look all through the book.

Index